Trace
Elements

TRACE ELEMENTS

Ted Pearson

Tuumba Press

ISBN: 978-1-931157-15-5

First edition, first printing

Some of these poems first appeared in *Lute and Drum*.

Text and Cover Design and Typesetting: Derek Fenner

Cover Art: Barnett Newman, "Untitled 2", 1949
oil on canvas; 24 x 28 1/8 in. (60.96 x 71.44 cm)
San Francisco Museum of Modern Art, Gift of Annalee Newman
© 2019 The Barnett Newman Foundation / Artists Rights Society (ARS),
New York. photo: Ian Reeves

Tuumba Press

Distributed by:
    Small Press Distribution
    1341 Seventh Street
    Berkeley, California 94710-1403
    www.spdbooks.org

CONTENTS

DOUBLE VISION

the function of Language is not to inform, but to evoke

– Jacques Lacan

for Barrett Watten

1.

Mute speech opens with a terse preamble.
Spurned hands languish in the doorjamb of doubt.

Infinity vents in all dimensions.
Eternity reckons no time at all.

2.

To logic's enchantment, I am no slave.
The music of things isn't scored in staves.

A series presents a moving target.
Abstractions revel in tawdry displays.

3.

Fault-lines are wary of ontic splinters.
Intangibles lust after bound morphemes.

Narcotic delights want proper fractions.
Topology glosses a nascent rift.

4.

A fallible gaze sweeps a fallow field
To map best guesses onto future yields.

With syllables subject to body counts,
We must scour their ambit for orphans.

5.

Lord Pan parties with honkytonk angels.
Oligarchs woo coquettes by the numbers.

A downbeat demiurge deploys tableaux
Reminiscent of somebody's slumber.

6.

"There's nothing more," said the doctor, "to say."
So why not lay off a few weeks, then quit?

Chaste nature repopulates the landscape.
Pillow talk smothers delusions at dawn.

7.

Narrative falsifies the storied brain.
Syntax has me at a disadvantage.

Circumspection may yet be a virtue.
The natives are hardy, but skeptical.

8.

Ancient Eros approaches his dotage,
Far from humble, but not "too proud to beg."

Love's true beneficence isn't a test.
Fantasies fortify workaday dregs.

9.

Monumental cultures encrypt the past
In lasting homage to the God of Stone.

What elders recall, the young reinvent.
Having come this far, they are on their own.

10.

Conduction brings new work into being.
Names are parcels that accommodate curves.

A gap appears between what we have seen
And what we think to say of what we saw.

11.

Buzzwords blur what they presume to define,
A distinction lost on the laity.

Human finitude includes bon vivants
Who are too preoccupied to notice.

12.

Method was once the new mythology.
Transcendental blossoms wilt in the sun.

While friendship weathers an affective chill,
The forest reverberates with silence.

13.

A heathen's heaven bestirs believers
While ethicists chant their anathemas.

Civil speech yields to hysterical chaff.
The imperium thrives on misprision.

14.

Sacrifice translates a lethal cliché.
Don't buy the lie if you can't pay the price.

Where risible precepts importune clowns,
Idlers cull virtue from notional vice.

15.

Locals dote on the station-master's wife
Whose beauty is ceaselessly arriving.

Shibboleths may well resent the present,
But not for its youthful indiscretions.

16.

Alternate canons deracinate trolls.
Grammar stocks up on its blithe exceptions.

Thus spake the mother of deprivations:
Recite your salad. Fuck your joie de vivre.

17.

History's mysteries, voiced from the grave.
I remember the day the author died.

Tiny flags waved atop colored map pins.
The statuary bled from its hinges.

18.

Austerity calls for heavy weather.
The open city was closed for repairs.

Cognates bristle at the sound of taboos
Whose acolytes labor in fetid air.

19.

An organon born of suppressed desire
Scraps tradition for the kinship of nods.

The fateful flames of chance operations
Engulf the white sail of our unconcern.

20.

A homeless man in the library stacks
Examines with care *The Wealth of Nations*.

His findings lead him to divagations
On the bounty to be had from dumpsters.

21.

Indigenes vet the empire's credentials.
Mountains rise up against weaponized rain.

Searchlights dismantle romantic shadows.
Manacles earmark the music of chains.

22.

Autobiography tempts the shredder.
Poverty's more than the absence of wealth.

Verisimilitude addles outcomes.
Blind fate determines the hand you'll be dealt.

23.

Lexical moonshine illumines our hootch.
Actual nooks and make-believe crannies.

A sudden surge has fried the motherboard.
Unforgiving is the coin of the realm.

24.

Metalanguage says what you meant to say.
Aging ascetics brake for mirages.

Think what you will. It's down to diligence.
My mood elevator just bottomed out.

25.

Portraiture preys upon living subjects.
The logic of sleep keeps dreams on the move.

Ten digits source an artful contrivance.
A cold sweat signifies something to prove.

26.

History absolves impenitent art.
Relationships end in parallel lines.

Ghost riders buttonhole brazen poppies.
Weasel words colorize upmarket crimes.

27.

Day labor sets its clock to a grindstone.
Line workers languish in mind-numbing tasks.

Synergy signals some slick semantics.
Ownership offers much less than it asks.

28.

A dissident choir sings dissonant odes.
At home in the gloaming, they speak in rimes.

Eidetic dreams suture shredded nerves.
Sound is asleep in the passage of time.

29.

By degrees, subjectivity lays bare
The person. This is its social command.

Capital's calculus, safe from remand,
Says parity leads to precarity.

30.

Imagine channeling actual bliss.
Autonomic writing, they meant to say.

Astral wonders follow after twilight's
Technicolor segues and slow dismount.

31.

Sheet lightning predates the cinema.
Pedagogic theory is stems and seeds.

A classic quintet seeks confirmation.
Cthonic changes transmogrify the scene.

32.

Angels cannot breed in captivity.
The hellhound sleeps by the gates of the Real.

Stress fractures outline bounds of affection.
Invisible wounds are the last to heal.

33.

A muscular thought strikes a sexy pose,
A look that panders to the pulse police.

The brokerage down by the crossroads says
There's a surfeit of souls for sale or lease.

34.

Street cred battles a textbook to a draw.
The present is woke to the lies of the past.

Now is the time to confront the monsters.
The body count from their havoc is vast.

35.

Billboards advocate personhood for hire.
Warrantless privilege fits like a glove.

Dead souls wander the streets of the city.
Wankers in wing-tips make rain from above.

36.

Predicates watch over subjects at play
Lest fouled lines hinder the catch of the day.

The middle voice sings of the middle way
Where the text is its own best example.

37.

Extinctions lead to deep ecology.
The Fates have repaired to their homemade world.

Variations are elaborations
Of the sites on which they are constructed.

38.

Permanent exile remains an option.
I is nothing but an instance of *I*.

By my count, we've lost more than a weekend.
Something a wise man would keep to himself.

39.

Rimes abound, infernal and inconstant.
A bald descriptor's a tough nut to crack.

M's deep cleavage divides the alphabet.
The B-side is strictly instrumental.

40.

Hyperborean breezes seize the day.
Anxiety's pennants flutter and flap.

There is forbearance. And there are regrets.
And it's then you become a memory.

41.

Dilations diminish in afterglow.
It's only what's under your hand that counts.

Call a gyre *prototypical desire.*
Accept that your resumé has no bounce.

42.

Language rewards its early adopters.
Right now, I just feel like humming a tune.

When fissures in feeling suborn the script,
Fatigued brains wither under mordant wit.

43.

Signification is on vacation.
"The arbitrary is meant to be sensed."

History stockpiles these emanations
Whose half-lives measure successive events.

44.

Where time is the torture that shapes their grief,
Review protocols for human subjects.

The social body is in constant flight,
But not necessarily from madness.

45.

Worn patches are mementoes of passage
From spanking new resolve to threadbare fate.

Contraltos sort these arias into
Genres of erotic maledictions.

46.

The virtue of clarity is to be
As clear as possible and no clearer.

My other is but my self divided
By a lifetime of corrosive labor.

47.

We went in search of coherent splendor
And settled for threads of random glory.

Aimless pleasures always hit their targets.
Libertine delights are yours for a song.

48.

Outliers rattle linguistic cages,
But what would writing be like without us?

Destitute tropes tell of life on the ropes,
In between dustbins and placards of yore.

49.

A dying star makes a splendid array.
"The medial landscape is instructive."

With the future of language up for grabs,
Unsung idioms remain seductive.

50.

Pathogens lurk in incunabula.
Ideation shelters in bold lemmas.

One is not one to complain, but one does.
I assure you this is not a sales call.

51.

Every frame seeks its vanishing point.
Surely not, states a structure by design.

Workers retreat in a stream of headlights
To sleep in the universal suburb.

52.

When open conflict constitutes the field,
Wildflowers rarely escape rendition.

How else account for the aura that glows
On the verge of a series in decay?

53.

Decoder rings are rarely mistaken.
I is unstable, if ready-to-wear.

Atonal clusters lounge on the drill ground,
Dolorous gleanings from the twilit air.

54.

Headlines foster attention deficits.
Irregular verbs are obsessed with the past.

Bitter tears follow on bitter insights.
Posthumous works are the ones that last.

55.

Skewed ratios are multiplexed buzz kills.
Prophylactic cover bands want for heft.

Uncertainties only mate in season.
A divining rod spurns a troubled cleft.

56.

Ululant cries signal dire misgivings.
The ship of state wallows in massive swells.

Shore-dwellers sing to the incoming tide
Enigmatic shanties with tales to tell.

57.

"Poor as dirt" is a social idiom
With nowhere to be and nothing to do.

The city's syntax is diegetic.
My squat is a blight on his scenic view.

58.

Tourists check off the Museum of Tears.
Then they retire to their rooms for the night.

The mockingbird tests the acoustic morn
With myriad variants, cool and bright.

59.

Eros amplifies noetic desires.
Factitious rivals have since interbred.

The chill in the room has rendered it moot.
Was it his silence or something he said?

60.

Structures instantiate daft ideas.
That's how they scale up our works and our days.

While first things meditate on what comes next,
The purity of ciphers still holds sway.

61.

Mixed strata are assumptions of beauty.
The crystal skull says, *We have ignition.*

Overclocked workers search the city for
The child's lost feeling of omnipotence.

62.

Magic is all about misdirection.
Embodiment shields us from open time.

Overtones occupy negative space.
Whispers at vespers revisit their prime.

63.

"A stream of particulars" runs its course
Over bedrock riven by seismic kinks.

When part-songs aggregate, close to the brink,
The Sphinx is a question, not an answer.

64.

Where nothing went missing, nothing was lost.
Time is restored when the odes reach their end.

I manage my symptoms by thought control
With the help of imaginary friends.

FOUR IN ONE

(death, / winter / and so on)

– Jackson Mac Low

for Lyn Hejinian

One

1.

Beyond our ken is a utopian premise.
Scattered motifs embrace their lot.
Real time wants you to support its assumptions.
Invisible lines seek evental release.

2.

The ideal reader is the author function.
Ontology outlines a change of scene.
Definitions follow from what they define.
Each next word is your last.

3.

Poverty absorbs contingent labor.
Any such thing asks just how much.
Today is an island in a growing chain
Of islands that I'll never see again.

4.

Collapsing stars make stunning backdrops.
Bygones litter the atrium floor.
Obsessives insist on revisiting their data.
Innings pass without a score.

5.

Notions crystallize around bold zippers.
The question *is* what the evidence means.
The brain's plasticity is omnisexual.
Woodland creatures are trending Green.

6.

Silence stays a well-versed tongue.
Noise is the prayer of the restless and young.
We broke an axle on the road less traveled,
Then hitched a ride to perdition.

7.

A drama unfolds between deep notches
In the bonds that define your ambit.
Sketchbooks filled with extreme renditions
Invite you to own your face.

8.

Audible audits quarry these stories
Of rare earth elements, out of their depth.
Things fall apart at the make-work factory.
An octave "leaps with credulity."

9.

What lantern for company or comfort
Among the so-called dead of night?
The spirit of darkness abides with me.
An asterisk isn't a prayer wheel.

10.

Buzzed cuts edit thinning locks.
Fictions are steeped in tales of the tribe.
Fortune's figments alight on walls
Where images of images are hung.

11.

A vernacular breeze sweeps tillable acres.
The rich assume their impregnable lives.
Surrealist canvases populate the windrows.
Exempla flee their concretion.

12.

Specters of guilt debilitate dreamers.
Chronic lust suborns their desires.
Sleep is a pseudonym for sweaty bodies
Strewn in wanton disarray.

13.

My days consist entirely of mornings
On the spooky shoals of consciousness.
Where destitution is a destination,
To deplore one's fate is to claim it.

14.

A change of clothes is a change of mind.
The hellhound sleeps in deep weeds.
Morbidity warrants a fresh round of carping.
One voice leads to another.

15.

The body in pain dispels the night.
Nothing but should nothing be.
Death arrives by terminal degrees
As if no other world were possible.

16.

Thought-lines crease the prisoner's brow.
An escape clause appears to be missing.
He dreamt of navigating moonlit curves
And woke with his head in his hands.

Two

17.

The low ghost rides the dissembling air.
Death is the work of a moment.
Factitious emotions spur our disdain.
A cleavage runs through existence.

18.

The shredder's a mode of assimilation.
Exile awaits our arthritic gait.
As soon as the morning fog burns off,
It's time to count the gargoyles.

19.

The threshold opened on a deep blue cipher.
A midnight ramble was his tithe to chance.
Unbridled passion requires no grooming.
Do you know the words to "My Romance"?

20.

Plot the pulse to line the beats.
Arpeggiation is strewn form.
Opposed pistons mime the tide.
Dance like your life depended.

21.

Some seek heaven in hell's despite.
I seek the languor of smoky dives.
Where aging poets perch on barstools,
"Fast falls the eventide."

22.

Rapid data spans your sight-lines.
A longue durée reinstates the nonce.
Canonical art surrenders at sunrise.
The wages of sin are its praxis.

23.

Roots instinctively probe foundations.
Small slights wallow in explanatory lags.
Unerring silence at the heart of song
Suggests the lyrics might be wrong.

24.

Picture windows are impervious to pain
Because what they frame is a fiction.
Eternity backlights the end of the tunnel.
A perfect match smolders in the dark.

25.

Stresses underscore cadenced orature.
Unbound morphemes flood the brain.
A synapse longs for a stable platform.
Meaning is chronically late for the train.

26.

The band laid out on the featured number,
A stunning solo at the cusp of thought.
Knowledge filters through the flux of things.
Specific losses are like as not.

27.

Erotic triggers lock down percepts.
Classic bell curves cost a bunch.
He whose writings are a sea of troubles
Heads for harbor on a hunch.

28.

Raptors roost in repurposed cities.
Foreclosures foment fear and blight.
Red lines border whatever remains
Of a populace driven to flight.

29.

The space she dreams is a proposition.
Its proof resembles the law of skin.
Chimeras lurk behind closed doors.
Endearments activate the tumblers.

30.

The snow line stays above the valley.
Shortened days are of a piece.
Much like anyone with something to prove,
The north wind howls like a beast.

31.

Xenophobes have no sister cities.
Irony supplements common travails.
You can't drown twice in the same river.
This we interpret to mean.

32.

Antique structures people ghost towns.
A shackle's logic extends down the years.
The text is at pains to retire its debts.
The End is a premise, not a threat.

Three

33.

My words regard me as an understudy.
Departures from normalcy are on the hour.
Epiphanies liberate makeshift genres
By which we disambiguate the tourists.

34.

Delusions run riot in early spring
Like so many tales of renascence.
Orpheus, for one, is tired of waiting.
And besides, his radio is broken.

35.

Its past has cost this moment its future.
Modes of production are tightly wrapped.
Consonant with its own conclusion,
The present is fickle if loathe to adapt.

36.

Eccentric mergers make bold anachronisms.
Cloistered walls house mythical beasts.
Survivors cleave to the roots of disaster.
The scent of evil troubles our sleep.

37.

Drought refutes the theology of lawns.
The threat to proper names is real.
Landscapes occupy aesthetic distance,
Whence their descriptive calm.

38.

The patient remained with his body
While new lines of code were installed.
Rejection would be the wiser counsel
In a world not far from this one.

39.

We've synched your scent to a bold locution,
A statement that cannot include itself.
But, once your body-double enters rehab,
We'll pull a bottle off the shelf.

40.

Corporate logos punch up the skyline.
The sun also rises on acres of lack.
The city you loved has burned its sources.
Lively scenes that you'd like back.

41.

In transition – from dust to dust –
Successive limits mark your advance.
You will have been writing your epitaph
When the future imperfect arrives.

42.

Jump cuts mime the turn to language.
Threadbare theatrics litter the page.
Zero probability is damned good odds
That you'll last till the final fade.

43.

Contested borders take migratory pulses.
Dancers rappel down invisible ropes.
Your fantasies need to keep their shirts on.
Denial is a violence done to hope.

44.

Today's glitches are tomorrow's ballistics.
The fruits of war are bitter indeed.
Our premises occupy vacant forms
Whose rhythms pace our needs.

45.

Imaginary elegies stage their preferments.
Legends languish on legendary maps.
Permanent crisis is the ultimate enjambment.
An irresolute architecture, mostly gaps.

46.

Causality balks at the least excuse.
A stiff wind braces an imaginary sum.
Oracles are a beneficence of stones
That weep, but only when it rains.

47.

Gang tags decorate the shuttered mall.
When did the neighborhood become a franchise?
Suspended sentences drift through the streets
In a modish ode to sociopathy.

48.

With its subjects prone to devolution,
A trackless waste is a source of fear.
When the only solution is dissolution,
The choice is to leave or be disappeared.

Four

49.

His obit reads like an exit interview.
Cause of death was acute ennui.
The sun shone down like a eulogy
To cover his nakedness with light.

50.

Stringent crystals bedeck the networked
Boughs that flourish on insurgent trees.
Transitional moments are ripe for seduction,
Whose terms of art are fallible.

51.

Edenic dreams were collateral damage.
The Muse has survived another white night.
Synaptic mordents grace these psalms
To laud the gods of squalor.

52.

Heart's ease summons an earlier era.
Last week's password was *epistemic grief.*
Reception amounts to a wintry silence
In the lives of deciduous pages.

53.

Dasein's motto is *Prepared to be.*
Lurid outcomes belie your beliefs.
Strange attractors gather wayward worlds.
Dreaming affords symptomatic relief.

54.

Rain clouds empty themselves of themselves.
Wind songs wind through a cavern's seams.
Drafts and fragments sweep the galleries.
Night and day are one.

55.

The dew point rises long after dark.
Illusions blur the edge of the frame.
It's time to revisit the broken mirror
Whose shards are your back pages.

56.

The Sirens want for binding arbitration,
But the metrics say our numbers are up.
Fantasts are flocking to sponsored content
Since we lashed Ulysses to the masthead.

57.

Libidinous poses are found wanting.
The hellmouth speaks of fire and ice.
Where trauma acts as a multiplier,
Shrieks of abstraction flee the page.

58.

Few dare follow the map that leads here.
The puzzle's complete when no pieces remain.
The margin of error has shrunk overnight.
Double vision isn't second sight.

59.

A pillar of files fights repatriation.
Nativists spew their viscid swill.
Cannibals thrive in communal foxholes.
Blood money stirs the political will.

60.

Species sing their songs of attrition.
Nature signs off on another extinction.
In the final version of our fall from grace,
The forecast is inclement weather.

61.

Parrots mouth mendacious claims.
Demonology is on the rise.
Vipers nest in ballot boxes.
A failed state frolics in imperial guise.

62.

Plangent music sweeps the dance floor.
Now there's nowhere for the ghosts to hide.
The ethical turn has had its moment.
Too few paragons yet abide.

63.

I pinned my career to an endless disclaimer.
Thoughts at ebb tide flow to the sea.
I still remember the taste of her kiss.
The train I ride is the train she missed.

64.

A bitter wind sweeps a bitter world
With a melody few could reprove.
It's not yet dawn in the present tense.
A score is an image of air on the move.

TRANSIENT GRAPHS

The wires in the rose are beautiful.

– Jack Spicer

for Carla Harryman

1.

Images are the business of poets whose work cannot benefit from Imagism. The music the poet hears with his eyes is the score that he plays in his head.

2.

Connections between words are invisible but true. Proof of concept is good to go. Consider the river that runs to the sea, at one with its restless murmurations.

3.

The stowaway dreams of the strangers she will walk among. She fears and longs for them in equal measure. On waking, she cannot distinguish her fear from the longing that underlies it.

4.

New knowledge wants new pages. Rare is the thought that escapes those habits of mind that typically precede it. Writing renders such thinking visible. "The outcome is thought, preserved."

5.

Your manifesto accords with our floor plan, whose keywords were borrowed from legends. They tell us who you wish you were and where you'll be when you are.

6.

Darkness her cloak and silence her refuge, the stowaway has fashioned a style. She is reading a history of bespoke disasters in a language foreign to her ear.

7.

Mental states pay value-added tax on the private languages they
think with. The locals are agog with thick descriptions of the lifestyle
they imagine to be yours.

8.

Strangers are widely viewed as strange. When asked to present her
passport, the stowaway bared her scars. If the new you is the new
normal, the old us is history.

9.

Meaning bestowed by syntax on experience was nursed back to
health by its mother tongue. When your sinecure depends on their
good graces, what you can't tell your elders is anything.

10.

A regatta of unison octaves swamps a raft of passing chords. Where
random access is a game of fetch, heliotropes are rhetorical figures in
the garden of common time.

11.

The text stays true to its retrograde motion, but turning to look isn't
given to see, unless and until it sees. Our last embrace was redolent
with smoke from the smoldering campfires of exile.

12.

As each word's a torment, each is a gift to enhance our collection of
imaginary numbers. Above which hope like a fine mist hovers, but
burns off well before noon.

13.

Come to play or stay away. Current strategy requires participation.
It's all a matter of timing. She had a chair, but no place at the table,
so she laid her cards on the air.

14.

As past gains drain into present losses, tell us your telos and we'll date
your demise. We have it right here in the Book of Desires. There's a
chapter devoted to you.

15.

Biography isn't destiny, unless that's how you play it. But that guitar
is missing strings you never knew it had. So what exactly does
experience teach and when exactly does it teach it?

16.

A benighted nation grows weary of its marvels. The underworld wakes with an eye to the weather. It's time for Orpheus to change his sheets. The springtime of language is at hand.

17.

Drawn to the vacuum between beauty and estrangement, you wonder which choices are truly yours. And what of the interior (it might be your own) that fades without gathering depth?

18.

The tighter the roll, the slower the burn. Recurring tropes accelerate decryption. Intimate gestures follow hard on the transitory contours of presentness.

19.

The stowaway marvels at young lovers who occupy the heat of their moment. Neither shall they want for unabashed kisses or an eagerness for all things flesh.

20.

A crop of creatives, jonesing hard. Survivors will pass for reasonable doubts. When irony blankets your local bar, the regulars will be priced out.

21.

Life without dreams invites psychosis. The last frost killed off the family tree. No instance is distinct from its setting. *For instance* signals a change of scene.

22.

The sexes hanker for gendered outcomes. All the sexes. Every gender.
Behind these masks is more than one seems. You can find your way
home from here.

23.

These equations unlock the mysterium. To be alive is to be undone.
Same message. New sender. Who seeks to finish ahead of her time
will have left no forwarding address.

24.

It takes more than solicitude to offset volatility. Defenses stand or fall
on their merits. The death merchants call this "the kill zone." Our
elders called it Fate.

25.

Allusions flatter the connoisseur, but must hold true for the work at hand. Most of the stowaway's stolen moments were lessons in how to read.

26.

Talking to her is like talking to yourself, or would be if you spoke in tongues. When words become things you must trust to your wits and remember to take your medications.

27.

An imponderable speaks to a degree of difficulty. Today's standing order is "Suppress the text." So much depends on the arc of sublimity, but nothing feasible survives this plane.

28.

Language *is* the event or there isn't one. That's why the stowaway spends her nights hooking up with mismatched symptoms. Suffice to say, they've had their fun, and they've got the scars to prove it.

29.

An extravagant beauty executes etudes with metronomic hips. Then we repair to the Temple of Doubt where a stiff drink smooths out wrinkles in the unsized fabric of time.

30.

In the parting words of Irascible the Elder, lose the attitude and eat your greens. The path to satori is strewn with dissertations. Closed casket. Family and friends.

31.

The poet is ever estranged from the poem. Not what you wanted to hear. Causality once was the Prince of Causes. Now, it's a junkyard of limited effects, defined by what they are not.

32.

Penitential glances find make-work everywhere. A thread on social justice leads to the merits of Cuban cigars. Between the front porch and an old blue law, Sunday morning passes.

33.

Public discourse is below grade level. Dharma compliance is in single digits. Sentient beings slumber in droves. It's time to rouse them with cadenzas.

34.

For those who walk these haunted halls, the brutal do more than just "act out." Probability besets us with known flash points. The poem's first language is asleep.

35.

The dimensions of the mind he inhabits predate the reason that it's cheap to rent. Now he constitutes a populace of one that didn't previously include him.

36.

Artlessly arrayed in a common grave, the intertwining logics of worlds. We can say of an image, it desires to be seen, but that doesn't mean we want to see it.

37.

Form is more than a silent witness to whomever would hold it harmless. Even as options shrink with age, a book, once bound, has depth.

38.

Who engineered the first quandry? Who knew that chance had whims? If knowledge is the threshold of the great unknown, what do we know when we get there?

39.

Priorities magnetize your passionate resolve. Intensities fade on a day like any other. Once in a blue moon, realism prospers. *Fine by me*, says the poet.

40.

Obliquity's a dialect, not a language. You didn't have to be here, and you still don't. Light is but one consequence of fire. Praxis is another. Feel the burn.

41.

The word made flesh was a metaphor from jump street. It's hard to sit through these family romances. History is an epic that includes poetry. Must it always be *your* family?

42.

A ghost has adopted the third person. The stowaway's narrative exceeds her grasp. She has the story well in hand, but not, as it happens, the telling.

43.

There must be more to mimesis than greasepaint. Comparisons pale
with repetition. More than once, having lost our way, we survived on
grammar and duct tape.

44.

The defeat that his passion for exactitude must suffer doesn't mean
that *he* must suffer. This is called aesthetic distance. An exercise in
mental geography.

45.

Language remains a tough sell, so you have your gods and your
dreams. Tables of values befuddle the sage. Death cuts short the
digressions of age.

46.

The poet's mind is a system of caves in which every grotto is a new world, every strophe a catastrophe. That's why we never send him for coffee. The sunlight would only confuse him.

47.

Memories balk at the pain of forgetting. Do they need more structure than such pain affords? Of this was told a tale of the world that arose at the end of the world.

48.

The poet dwells among his books, which form his last redoubt. They are as mirrors when he looks within and greets the startled dead looking out.

Ted Pearson (1948) was born and raised in Palo Alto. He began writing in the mid Sixties and has since authored twenty-four books of poetry; co-authored *The Grand Piano*, a ten-volume experiment in collective autobiography, and co-edited *Bobweaving Detroit: The Selected Poems of Murray Jackson*. Recent works include *Personal Effects* (BlazeVOX) and *Exit Music* (Singing Horse). He lives in Oakland, California.

Trace Elements
was printed in an edition of 500 copies
at McNaughton & Gunn.
Text and cover design and typesetting by Derek Fenner
using Adobe Garamond.